Little Bible Heroes™
Creation

Written by Victoria Kovacs
Illustrated by Mike Krome

B&H
KIDS
NASHVILLE, TENNESSEE

GOLDQUILL
WWW.GOLDQUILL.CO.UK

Published by B&H Publishing Group 2015. Text and illustrations copyright © 2014, GoldQuill, United Kingdom.
All rights reserved. Scripture quotations are taken from the Holman Christian Standard Bible ® Copyright © 1999, 2000, 2002, 2003, 2009 by Holman Bible Publishers. Used by permission. Printed in Heshan, Guangdong, China, January 2019
ISBN: 978-1-4336-8712-9   Dewey Decimal Classification: CE
Subject Heading: CREATION \ NOAH \ BIBLE STORIES
6 7 8 9 10 11 12 • 23 22 21 20 19

In the beginning, God created everything. On the first day, He said, "Let there be light." On the second day, God made the sky.

On the third day, God made the oceans and the land. He also made the grass and plants and trees to grow.

On the fourth day,
God made the sun
and moon and stars.

On the fifth day, God made birds and all the creatures that live in the sea.

On the sixth day, God made all the animals on the earth. He also made Adam and Eve, the first people.

God looked at what He had made.
It was a good new world.

On the seventh day, God rested from all His work. His creation was finished!

Read:

In the beginning God created the heavens and the earth.—Genesis 1:1

Think:

1. God created the whole world. What do you like to create?
2. What is your favorite thing that God made?

Remember:

The heavens are Yours; the earth also is Yours. The world and everything in it— You founded them.
—Psalm 89:11

Read:

Then the LORD said to Noah, "Enter the ark, you and all your household, for I have seen that you alone are righteous before Me in this generation."—Genesis 7:1

Think:

1. Would you like being on the ark with Noah and the animals?
2. God always keeps His promises. Have you ever made a promise?

Remember:

"I will remember My covenant between Me and you and all the living creatures: water will never again become a flood to destroy every creature."
—Genesis 9:15

God puts the rainbow in the sky as
His promise that He will never again
flood the earth.

Noah and his family and all the animals leave the ark. Noah builds an altar to God. He thanks God for saving their lives.

Everyone on the ark is waiting and waiting. The ground will soon be dry.

Noah sends out a dove. The dove returns with an olive leaf. That means the water is finally going down!

Once all the animals and Noah's family are in the ark, God makes it rain for forty days and nights.

God tells Noah to build an ark. The ark is taller than a three-story building! Noah brings animals into the ark.

Noah is a righteous man and does what God says to do. But the other people on earth are bad. That makes God sad.

Little Bible Heroes™
Noah

Written by Victoria Kovacs
Illustrated by Mike Krome

B&H KIDS
NASHVILLE, TENNESSEE

GOLDQUILL
WWW.GOLDQUILL.CO.UK

Published by B&H Publishing Group 2015. Text and illustrations copyright © 2014, GoldQuill, United Kingdom.
All rights reserved. Scripture quotations are taken from the Holman Christian Standard Bible ® Copyright © 1999, 2000, 2002, 2003, 2009 by Holman Bible Publishers. Used by permission. Printed in Heshan, Guangdong, China, January 2019
ISBN: 978-1-4336-8712-9   Dewey Decimal Classification: CE
Subject Heading: CREATION \ NOAH \ BIBLE STORIES
6 7 8 9 10 11 12 • 23 22 21 20 19